The Ocher of Abundance

The Ocher of Abundance

Poems

VOLUME 16

Wendy E. Slater

The Ocher of Abundance
Copyright © 2020 by Wendy E. Slater
Second Edition: January 2020
traduka.com

All rights reserved. No part of this book may be reproduced in any form or by any means, electronic or mechanical, including photocopying, recording, or by any information storage and retrieval system, without permission in writing from the publisher.

Wendy E. Slater books are available for order through
Ingram Press Catalogues

Traduka Publishing
traduka@traduka.com

Paper ISBN: 978-1-943512-20-1
E-book: 978-1-943512-21-8

BOOK DESIGN BY STREETLIGHT GRAPHICS
AUTHOR PHOTO BY JEFF WOODWARD
COVER PHOTO BY WENDY E. SLATER

For the Truth
And
The Path
To it

Invocation for Peace

TOGETHER let us hold the intention that all aspects of this living planet come together in love, acceptance, and celebration of both our diversities and commonalities. Let us possess the common purpose that we heal from our hearts into compassion and forgiveness for ourselves. Together let us own the belief that we will no longer unite with blame and judgment, but come to accept that we all carry the same wounds. In acknowledging this, the hope is for the whole planet in its jubilant diversity to be healed from any and all woundings so that we come together on equal footing, living in peace and joy and setting the tone for a future of harmony within and on this planet.
Peace to all and healing to all.

CONTENTS

Invocation for Peace .... *vii*

1601   In the stillness 1

1602   Full moons 2

1603   Hope and waiting 4

1604   It has been so long 5

1605   The oddness 6

1606   What is paved between 7

1607   Do I know you 8

1608   A sultry night 9

1609   The bleeding lip 10

1610   What is in the lack 11

1611   Spring's dance in the heart 12

1612   The plants are potted 27

1613   An echo of remembrance 28

1614   Shriveled 29

1615   Destroyed 30

1616	The holy passage	31
1617	The passage	32
1618	When did obsession	34
1619	When did uncertainty	35
1620	Where is my father	36
1621	The saddest tethered children	37
1622	Once upon a time	38
1623	Listening to an orator	39
1624	The most golden treasure	40
1625	A whispered lullaby	43
1626	I do not join with another	44
1627	What is the recalibration	45
1628	Radiant being	46
1629	The violation	47
1630	To give the being	48
1631	What is it	49
1632	Stress is stress	50
1633	Wayward and blown	51
1634	If your sweetness	52
1635	Obsession carves a home	53
1636	What is in	59

1637	In a breath and	60
1638	Come take me	62
1639	A kiss is a kiss	63
1640	What is untold Truth	64
1641	So, what was awakened	65
1642	Vague imprints	66
1643	In a dimensional	67
1644	Rooted and below	68
1645	If it all began	69
1646	The moonlit bliss	70
1647	Variegated winds	71
1648	Parameters of day and night	72
1649	No longer	73
1650	The expanse of golden	74
1651	The proper term for love	75
1652	In a random moment	77
1653	Germination	78
1654	Tendrils	79
1655	When perspective is peeled	80
1656	Abundance	81
1657	Witnessing in peace	83

1601

In the stillness
 Of the shuttered moment
 Is the grained texture of soul,
   Sight and sound
  As the framed aspect
     Folds into history
       Of imagined colors, radiant
      Exposure of light upon darkness,
        Shadows dappled into
         Filmed seemingly
           Transparent
            Dialogue
          Of truth and beauty,
            Elegance of whispered
             Artistry
            Linking eye to heart
            And palm
              With sometimes
               A scream
               Of ecstasy.

1602

Full moons,
   Tantric eclipses
     Linger no more,
     Neither in the palm, heart, eye,
        Nor in the unconfirmed
            Or confirmed echo and breath
              Of now and always
   Begins again
     As if it never ceased
       Nor stopped
       When foot folded
         Under the shadow
         Of it all.

A full moon
    In stilled water
    Is apparently
     Not the truth
    When you dive into
      And immerse in the illusion
      Bent by reflection,
        Arcs, trajectories
    Of spitting stars
       From breath
     To catch in the heart
        When footing is
           Unsteady.

A rose is always a rose
    In the garden, vase,
    Or wilted,
    Even folded back into the compost
     That has the revelation
       Of truth,

Not as a secret to unfold
    But in the touch
        Of the petal, stem,
        And even the thorn,
        With care.

1603

Hope and waiting
   As rightful seasoned
     Approach
Has been abandoned,
     Rather stolen
      By the touch
        Of my light against light,
       Betrayed by the guised
      Theft
        Of nothing else,
           I suppose,
       Than self.

It has been so long
　　Since love whispered
　　　　Through my hair
　　As the wind touching and licking
　　　　The exposed, skin under sun,
　　　　Appearance of stillness
　　　　　As the erotic dance
　　　　　　Unfolds.

1605

The oddness,
    The discordance
    Of not wanting
        A return to home,
Although the heart is here
  Now rested and at peace,
    Bedded and wedded
      Alone, seeded
        And ripened
        Into the peculiarity
        Of the knowing.

1606

What is paved between
    The heart and palm?
      Girlish giggles, sheer abandoned freedom
        Of voice, range, and depth,
        Sultry wind lifting grief from the brow.

The shift is knowing
      The attractive force
        And the disengagement
          Of a false destiny
          Bound to hostility, expense
            To bind the wounds,
              Keeping the peace
              Only to discover
                The untouched
                Rage
                  Feeding the hidden
                  Ambiguity.

1607

Do I know you
  Or me?
    Have I been bound
      In your vengeance
      Gilded with remorse,
         Resentment and deceit,
            Such that there could be
              No ownership
           Of self nor truth
             Until this all
                Came clear
                    Under a full moon?

1608

A sultry night
  Is full of daffodils,
A man with a cart and bedding,
    Luggage and grief,
   Wheeling and bumping,
      Singing a lonesome song
     Through the lot
        Trailing to no home
          Of hearth and walls,
         But to tracks,
           Tiredness and abandon.

1609

The bleeding lip
    Is bitter
    Hard ice,
        Folds of venom
        Hidden by the pocketed
            Deceit, deception
        Fanged into the lotus
            That held the love,
    Only to be mirrored
        By a jealous heart
    Incongruent
        With truth.

1610

What is in the lack
    Of control
    Of faculties?

1611

Spring's dance in the heart
      love's tender taste of sweet nectar
      sapling has become the warrior

Spirit's ecstasy trampled
      under frozen foot of thought
      resilience springs as heart sings

Exalted song of the night
      tendrils bring into light
      abundant glory of who I am

Lark's song trembles in the dawn
      as shield is dressed and sung
      and the dragon's flame dances

The arc of fallen stars
      brings to the awakened one
      triumph of who we are

Soft-footed steps
      yielding bounty, harvest and fruits
      of what has been seeded in the past

One generation, two, and three,
      home to home
      is hand to heart

Bow stretched and tensed
      as arrow flies in its song
      through sweet and salted breath

Having reached and even touched
      recoiled action springs to mind
      a picture of the time

The stem, stamen, and pistil
    came together to lament
    a fallen petal to ground

The bouquet was given
    wilted and then denied
    there was not time to cry

A hidden grief lays afield
    from flying timbers, mortar and the shells
    holding histories' battles as a monument

Today's lea is fertile
    from the known order of creation
    my forest is in sight

The owl cries in the dark
    to find the one it loves
    to remind the day that it will come

Swiftly flown feathers
    are sewn into a headdress
    ecstatic dance of who I am

The breath was given and not received
    and in that moment
    a bird comes home to nest

The golden truth of dawn
    with broken promises
    bleeding from exaltation

A stolen yard is timeless
    and in the gap
    it is all exposed

Raw, vulgar insanity
    denigration of truth
    falling into the foxhole

Mined back to self
>	and the gems
>	still in vain

What is gone
>	never began
>	as the moment never ceases

The crime of war
>	is not without horror
>	unveiled as a juvenile drunken disregard

Part truth, part lies
>	littered out like corpses
>	counting the dead to gain the advantage

To cover the hurt
>	like white sheets over open eyes
>	limbless and banged up

Cold-shouldered volunteers
>	swept under the tank
>	barbed fences in the self

All ploughed under
>	garden's bounty radiates even
>	where deceit and betrayal hold their song

I can be loved as the delicate tendril
>	the fierce warrior
>	and the sensual woman

Because home is home
>	the walls do speak
>	when we listen

There is always song
>	a labor of love
>	carries tears and joy

The breech birth has the ecstasy
    of bringing in the baby
    the miscarriage holds the longing

The dropped
    a hoped sweetness
    when a trust be known in the souring

Destiny unfolds whether
    the day is long
    the night is short

The stars still dance
    I now hear the ballad
    grieving for what my ears became deafened to

Blinded by hidden beauty
    responsible for bitter taste
    when all that happened was I sang my hallelujah

The awe of that descending star
    lightning striking boldness
    the courage to walk the path

To teach the lesson
    that has arrived
    like some long yawn

Silent no longer, alone no more
    hovering between despair
    and assassination of the self is absent

Aborted dreams to aid the other
    leaves the border not only
    neglected but invites the trespass

When the line is drawn, the country declared
    the hawk can soar over the arbitrary confines
    and the warbler raises its head

Makes its brood
        on your mountain
        in my home

Never scarred as it sings
        my song of love
        by the sea or in the weeds

Derelict amplitude of voice
        did not desecrate
        the lack of sound

The pardon for the sweetness
        allowed the coarseness to show
        its fangs

All the while
        pulling it forth
        so not to repeat the historic proportions of past

A mistake is never a mistake once
        it is twice along
        rather my whispers were to pull

All back to the cradle
        to the trust
        sweet lullabies to who I am

Who are you?
        philosophers will tell me
        troubling tales

The poet knows the sorrow
        the artist renders it back to canvas
        and the voice no longer swallows it up

A snifter of brandy
        lifts the wounded soldier
        from battlefield to amputation

The lost country is devoured by greed
        oil for the corporation
        uranium for the reaction

Innocence proclaimed from the energy
        complete without carbon footprint
        is the total claim

Wide-toothed lies with split tongue
        as before the reaction
        the processing renders pollutants

Completely traceable outline
        of guilt, deceit to keep one warm
        and in the light

When it was the shadow
        that rendered the absorption
        in first place nihilism created

After the greed, always after
        and before the firs stake
        planted next to

The snake hisses
        venom hidden and in plain view
        with recoil and fangs grinning

In the exposed moment
        the riddle undone
        echoes answered

Melancholy posing in the heart
        as destitution of soul
        rendered mute, silent without the grace

Of the swan on the pond
        in the soil and of the earth
        blossoms burst forth

Declaring spring before summer
      and the fall poised
         before it all hibernates

Back into the womb, the hearth
      to collect the trust
         the truth to put one step in front

The next is always helpless
      when it is uncertainty
         trusting is knowing every second

Collapses and rebuilds into the next
      the wave ebbs only to flow
         the heart cannot close

Love is love
      and the sight and sound are neither blind
         nor muted by the expansive shading of greed

Currency is forced to be amplitude
      of truth
         when poverty is never in the heart

But the pocket will not be full
      when definition of self
         is conquest and denigration

Of that which bore us:
      truth, love, and resilience
         wild adventure is saddled

Onto a blind horse
      that sees through the eyes
         of the rider

Neither reined nor bridled
      untamed and untethered
         celebrating the journey

To truth, orbiting the moon
> discovering the dream interpretation
> 5 years too late

And yet arriving just on time
> as the fluency of language
> was unknown to self

Hungry and indigestible was your touch
> sharing meals
> of deceptive tastes and textures

Living in a foreign land
> with languages and customs
> learned not just for survival

The secret agent lives with the enemy
> to restore justice and equanimity
> to liberate the downtrodden

So, fluency of my tongue
> can speak your idioms
> feign camaraderie with The General

In the army to fall
> the corporation to be revealed in deceit
> or the derelict with the heart

Only now as an explorer into
> the unspoken terrain
> has it been reclaimed

Not with arbitrary lines
> in soil mandated by the council
> but with a revelation

Of truth that was always there
> the sparkle is gone from the eyes
> too much sorrow and devastation

This angelic land has not been cherished
    by lips of innocence
    since before the Ice Age

Neanderthal man revealed
    touch imagined was coarse
    primitive but by that definition

Subtlety was felt as friction
    rock to rock
    sinew through lips

Neither today nor yesterday a sanctuary
    the heart longs to be held
    in the palm

As honor is nobler
    sweet cherishment liberates
    even the most scarred land

As the gardener touches
    the tendrils with gentle nourishment
    like love parched

Such that petal never stood before on stalk
    and bee never came to blossom
    honey was never created nor tasted

This land is not just pocked and dented
    an ordinary being would have gotten
    up and walked straight off the cliff

The pain of impact better
    than the implosion
    impact and collapse

The duration of this is surrender
    sometimes it was manipulation
    such that weighted strains

Could and would thrive
        in this withered wasteland
        too radioactive to touch

Untold story held in the breath
        as if then the poison could reach
        into the momentary gap

Of breath there is silent grief
        aberration of violation
        without expression

Density coupled into vacuous voids
        renders black holes
        only fathomed through intellect

And I miss the planet
        in its aimless orbit
        even the dangerous descent

Into madness that reached out
        and held me accountable
        for beauty, innocence and humility

As jealousy is the crime
        and without it in the vocabulary
        there could be no trespass

The coveting took the sparkle
        developed the bomb
        and blew the radiance into too many

Directions to count and grasp
        fractions and fractals
        leave remnants of a woman that is not known

To be me is a passage untold and unavowed
        strength renders decisions masked
        veiled like a clown

Tears stumbled over untied laces
    heart broken from the fall
    distanced whispers fold into the sound

Nothingness is violent
    when it trembles the other
    into a lack of control

For there is no truth
    to the hollers, wails and whimpering
    straddling the line

The question is to die
    in unconquered land
    or in the enemy's hand

Secrets still cannot be touched or realized
    hierarchy is built on rotten timbers
    the angle all out of alignment

The call for truth is absolute
    and the wind falls between the fingers
    a solitary leaf neither completes

Nor joins the pile
    for the clump would be the same
    with or without

Hailing victories like some obsolete dictator
    in a too small country
    no more than a house

Began this tale
    of one fist
    into the other

Taking as entitlement
    blinds the children
    and binds the feet

The womb will not hold the child
        as if it was ever wanted
        but as a dream

Life would be different
        little feet in little shoes
        scraped knees kissed and loved

Teaching to heal and be free
        from life's treachery
        the common wound inflicted

From the beginning word by word
        of chapter into chapter
        and tome into tome

A library is filled
        and I miss my father's comfort
        the eyes and love

Never feeling orphaned nor alone
        nor mistaken as any other
        confusion was given clarity

The mother's charm, elegance, and artistry
        blend into a galaxy
        far from home I have always been

Friendship has eloped with deceit
        wanting to steal the bread
        not from hunger but to starve the soul

It is all traceless and knowing where
        it all began and ends
        leaves depressed imprints

Smudged fingerprints
        bruised marks
        and broken strings that no longer play

No one ever heard
      nor did they know
      the binding of the innocence

The spirit robbed
      the loot hoarded
      such that minstrels sound horns

Never seen nor known
      and play and dance
      celebrating the captive

Neither me nor you
      can see the story
      the sense of it all

Never to be loved
      again
      as I was

As that has disintegrated
      the dust creating new cosmic seeds
      to bring the truth back home

As rains and planets never known
      just now identified
      as the garden comes to life

Butterflies in flight
      engaged upon the breath
      hummingbirds' nectar filled

Daisies dancing with the strife
      violets sheltering pansies
      purple into purple

And of the light
      lupines seeded into soil
      columbines to come

Lilacs sweeping through the home
        forsythia meandering in the vase
        hidden treasures of winter's rest

Enthroned into the reign
        tiara with pistils and stamens
        gems of scents and musky lull

Sultry summer swinging
        barefoot from the tree
        plunging into ponds

Crystal reflection of what will be
        even when clouds distort
        depth of life

To be born
        is alone
        joined by breath

To love
        to see
        and touch

The golden roaring of the lion
        on the rock
        in plain sight

Proud and alive
        when in range
        it all cycles through

But has any eclipse ever been
        as alone
        and tampered with?

There is none
        to give into nor understand
        for nothing makes sense

Of it all
      or none
      or whispering in the ear.

1612

The plants are potted
   By the roadside,
    Wilted and evenly parched
      Desert path,
     Burnt soles,
    Flanged
     Without a drop
        To spare,
      And the heat
       Sears and grills
        As grief is breathing
       And bottled,
        Quenching without
          Recourse.

1613

An echo of remembrance
    Dances in shadows
        Of full moons
     And clenched in the fist
  Tethered kite to hand
       In the heart and now
  Sail heaved up to gust.

1614

Shriveled
   And having died
   A million deaths
   And gasps in the willowed winds
Gulping into a gap
   Free-fall
   And the chasm
   Seeming never to end
      But collapsing back
        Into again and again.

1615

Destroyed
   And wrecked,
Wondering if footing to the grounding
   Will never unfold.

When joy is touched
     With a fingertip to air,
  It is without taste and bland,
    No delicacy of flavor,
As the wind has not touched
    Nor warmed
      In ages.

Bound to stakes no longer
   As the old and decaying
   Withers on the post,
     One hand by the side
      Infected and nail
         Blistered into palm,
    The other waiting in the pause,
     Infected talons, beaked
       Soaring glints
        Of waiting to see
         Before the ego is eaten alive.

1616

The holy passage,
   Walled and bricked,
Mortared with disappointment and grief,
   Gluey despair in the breath,
   Cementing isolation
      To the point of confusion—
      Grounded in a perpetual pirouette,
         Pink tutu and pointe shoes,
Has it all been stolen?
        It is too dark to see
        If the audience left
          Or even cared.

1617

The passage
    A minute too late
      To carry the cargo,
    A minute too early
      To pretend to want to go
  The route
      Lacking touch, understanding
        And ecstatic joy
          In and for another.

Knowing veiled love
    Was already in mourning
    Like the old widow,
    The mobster's wife
      Who said she never knew
Yet looking too close,
    The grief became shadows
    To sweep away
      With a tender touch
    While the hand which should have
      Been clasped to palm
  Reached into
      The back pocket
        To steal with a toothless smile
          And feed
    The false cloak of innocence.

    And by right of passage,
    Legitimacy was granted
Such that veils sweeping over
    Became mined
    With the black garb
    And without the delicacy
      Of culture.

A wandering
        Gummy,
     Desolate truth
     Of shades and shapes
          Of the strapped arm
            And its veined course.

Obsession is falsely legitimized
        And a barren emptiness
          Of control
       Like the fierce Siroccan wind
          Raging into blindness
         And away
          Forever.

1618

When did obsession
    Knock the teeth out
    With one solid fist
        Left right
            Under the jaw?

A rocky road
    Bound
    For 18 years or so,
        Yoked and seamed
            To false truths
                Under the hem
                    Like weighted curtains,
                Too heavy to let
                    The breeze in
                    On a too hot summer's day.

And it is time to wonder
        If I should move
        And leave it all behind?

1619

When did uncertainty
    Become the enfoldment
    Of containment
    Into the open urn of love
        Which still holds
          Ash solidified,
            A pasted smear
              To paint the face
    And arch toward target
        Pinned to bull's-eye
          Waiting no longer
          As it is all done
            And
              Bled into despair
            Of the Path
            Being so mistaken
            And so nowhere
            Spiraling down
              And down
            The Yellow Brick Road.

1620

Where is my father
>   To blend his wisdom to me
>   And listen wholly of heart?
And in the willingness to be
>   A human
>   It is now known
>   There will be no children
>   None shall be.

1621

The saddest tethered children
    Scream up into the
    Open window,
Their pained cries,
    The same ones every day,
    And the hearts are broken
      Even before the house
        Comes apart.

Once upon a time
    There was joy in the unknown
        Mystery, the folded dots
        Into space and time;
    There was no need to
        Define as an Absolute
        Whether or not
          It was
        With direction and intensity.

        Now there is amplitude
       Such that uncertainty
      Is locked to failure
        Rather than springing
          With possibility,
    So disconnected,
        So very.

1623

Listening to an orator
Who has dedication
To an arena,
   A venue that requires
   Straps, stirrups
    And saddled to the horse,
    Hurled toward a false sun
       On a dark night,
  Only to stumble, hurtling off the cliff
      With nothing even to catch
         The fall and never
      To ground
        Again.

      All in a moment
        Faster than the eye
        Can blink
        I want to vomit.

1624

The most golden treasure,
    Me to myself,
  Is now tainted by another's
    Feigned interest as obsession
      With disregard
        For the sacrosanct.

Addiction
    Saddled into manipulating
    Anyone's vulnerability,
    Riding the horse
    Ass-backwards, barefooted
        And sweaty,
      Veins popping
          Waiting for the next jump.

 Never knowing how high
        The leap will be
          And where to land,
      There is no wonder
        One day if they will be cold and dead,
    The horse gleefully off to find
      Any other rider, as there
        Never was a loyalty.

The only uniform
            Was tracks
          In the parched,
       Scratch marks from all
          The dismembered
          Humping of the equine
        To become a by-product
           Of the donkey and horse: the mule
              To carry the load.

It is my body
>   That trembles
>   With uncertainty
>   When a friend vows
>   To have the horse
>   Out to pasture
> Yet, in that
>   They have become
>   The gold medalist
>   In the steeplechase.

This is my body, and I thank God
>   Most of them cannot even
>   Figure out how to
>   Pump it up
>   For anything
>   But the ride
>   Of the donkey, mule,
>   And horse.

Having said that,
>   I must say there is no
>   Care nor desire
>   To protect anyone
>   From HIV or Hep C,
>   As they think
>   We all must fall down.

There is nothing to say
>   Ever to one
>   Who has lied
>   Face-to-face
>   About the thing I hold
>   Most sacred: my body, my temple.

But the rage disarmed
>   The disgrace and veils
>   Of friendship
>   Such that
>   None shall trespass again.

And I shall ride a mustang of my own
               Without tracks and tethers,
            High into the hills
             To be closer
               To none other
               Than the beloved.

Blinded I was
              To believe truth and honesty
              Could come from one
              Whose choice is to hide
               Not only from amrita's essence
                But to denigrate and violate
                What I hold holy:
               Me.

1625

A whispered lullaby
    Like some soliloquy
        Of Shakespeare
  Is not present but ever timeless,
    The hourglass
      Measuring
      By endless strands
        Of despair
        From manipulation.

    The open-handed fist innocent
      While the other creeps
        Through the back pocket
        To the sacred dowry.

I do not join with another
   But reveal deeper
      To myself
     All of life's mystery
        Unfolding—
So in my distaste
   For what has
      Evolved,
 I must know and embrace
 It is all the revelation,
   The awakening,
    So that the Big Bang
   May unflower
   In permanent
   Radiance
 Of full moons, starry galaxies,
 Auspicious eclipses, all
From my truth,
    Always and now.

1627

What is the recalibration
    Of the heart?
Unsung densities
    And potentials
      Now revealed as nothing
        More than shadows framed
          And boxing in the umbra
        With pinhole openings of light
      Pretending to be a galaxy,
        Symphonic breath,
          And the hand of God.

The resung and remembered
      Truth emits out,
    No longer eclipsed
    With all the grasping, longings,
      Mistrust and grief
      Of the self
    Before the sail opens
      To soar through
        Light-years
          Of radiance's bounty.

🍃 1628

Radiant being
   In the gummy gap
 Receding into the ocean,
As obsessed ones,
     Coordinates on a sonar graphing,
      Wait for the implosion from the intersection
        In perpetuity of illusion.

        It never was,
          Never will be,
          As was
          Always told.

1629

The violation
　　Of dishonesty hovering
　　As desecration
　　　　Above the holy
　　　　Has resounded
　　　　Into the heavens
　　　　And out of the ocean
　　　　　　As thunderclaps
　　　　　　And seismic shifts
　　　　　　　　Of tidal waving
　　　　　　　　　Goodbye forever
　　　　　　　　　　As it never
　　　　　　　　　　　Was but a delusion.

1630

To give the being
    The noose
    To hang one's self
    Upside down
      In obsessive
        Suspension,
         Dormancy
       Like the bat
        Clinging,
         Waiting to fly.

1631

What is it
   That has died in me,
  Not as a bleeding
    Out but resurrected
     From the corpse
    And watching from
       Afar
     At high noon, full shadow
     Before the clouds came
     And the imprint left?

1632

Stress is stress
    Is stress,
  Sewn backwards,
     Waiting,
      Weighted,
        And belly up.

1633

Wayward and blown
    Up to the mountain
  In sight
     Which is why
       The move
         Occurred
          For now
            Peaceful footsteps
             And the tiger roars.

1634

If your sweetness
    Touched my lips
   In an Absolute
     Moment,
  The vulnerability
     Would reveal
    To be licked
       By the taste of all
         Always.

1635

Obsession carves a home
    far from heart
    a far-off place

Near to none
    as star to star
    repels the innocence

Of giving, gifting
    and gone
    spilt to grief

Betrayal of a darkness
    clouding, swelling
    to bring the rains

Such that tear to tear
    you make the tether
    that will now hold

You in place
    to touch in depth
    all that you feared

The truth is knowing
    the mirage of intimacy
    is now withered

Like a locust
    branch severed from the tree
    by scabbings

And the thorns
    fell from the sky
    into your heart

With the allegiance
      to none other
      than getting smacked

Again and again
      the brilliance bled
      into a puddle

Of spoons, belts
      with teeth marks
      discarded and used

Butt ends
      'cause you said
      you wanted to smoke

Them straight
      into your paradigm
      of the discordant

Disregard for Truth
      that trumpets up and out
      from the source of One

To believe and bind
      to this false sense of ecstasy
      sings like a lark

In the moment
      without treble, throat
      or winged flight

Never nested and without
      sense of honor
      or knighthood

The eunuch has replaced
      the union
      with divided

Urgency to string, strand
    and weave
    a web of tangled deceit

Unveiled like a corpse
    laid out to rest
    that has been dead

For too many years
    to count the lies,
    dishonor and blending

Of what was thought
    to be hearted friendship
    to empower

To recognize now
    the clock never moved
    and the day never came

Dawn was twilighted
    in the glassy eyes
    tilted perspective

Of being too weighted down
    standing atop the earth
    your head never hit the sky

And I was too generous
    with sight
    in seeing two sides

As now I am blended
    back into one
    finally so vulnerable

That love's breath
    may tickle me
    as the snow falls

Far from me now
> always you will be away
> and now I welcome

The treasure of knowing
> the heart can be held
> in the palm of the hand

In awe, love, and wonder
> all will appear
> not as a dream

But a warrior of armored love
> to defend and nourish
> his love: me

And the reason it could never
> ever be you
> as eunuch nor man

Nor even woman nor human
> is love is not possession
> nor obsession

Deceit and manipulation
> are addiction
> to destruction

Of self by selfishness
> such that aggrandizement engages
> like a rat

Roaring through
> the underbelly of ego's
> dance of seldom seen

Narcissism
> looking into the water
> noting nothing

But now the truth
        has split you open
        like an atom cleaved

From me
        and to you
        you must reap

What you have sown
        masquerading as loyalty
        in the jester's suit

Jack of diamonds, spades,
        clubs, and hearts
        do not make a deck

Nor platform to perform
        card tricks, hidden tracks
        unexplained scratches

Mapping a route
        of all the points, red and traced
        of where your needle has been

You would find
        no need for passport
        as you have gone

Nowhere at all
        but deeper into lies
        of stunning proportions

That lack structure, individuality
        and, yet, with a strength of the void
        that belongs to such

Darkness with neither dawn
        nor delight,
        artificial colors

Would not even thrive,
    as it is all too cold
    in this space.

1636

What is in
   Heaven's gate?
     Breath
       Beyond the known
         Exhale, inhale
           Passion of light
             To hold the dawn
               Of all that is known
               I love you.

1637

In a breath and
   A stare
With flutter of lids,
    What does one see?
Tiger with unfurled
      Claws
  In aggression.
Rather, it should be
 Tiger with claws
      Unfurling
 In passion of love
      And embrace.

So what is lost
     In the translation
 In the universe
    Of 2 planets
    Orbiting
    In perpetuity
    Until one
    Is swallowed
      Into the black hole?

A beacon of darkness
   Is not despair
  But transformation to the core.
Yet, it is all so alone,
     Truly explorative
Of regions never known,
  Galaxies tasted in a blink,
And to touch
    The seam of the heart
   Is all there is
    To this moment.

Arced back in triumph
    At nothingness,
Golden leaves
    Hiding the oblique
        Past—
And into one day
    As an archaeologist
It will all be told,
    Uncoded so
That nothing ever
    Makes sense
Except from sitting on
    A rock, on a hill
    At the sunset
     Of knowing only
      Then
    What the dawn
      And mourning
        Means.

1638

Come take me
    By the hand
  In the dark
    Between two full moons
      And dissonant dissolution
        Back into nothing,
          As if nothing was ever
There
    Is no history, no evidence
      To know
    And trust when it appears
      Again all because
        Of the forgetting,
      Fraught
        And taught
        To be
          As it never was
            Nor will be.

1639

A kiss is a kiss,
  But breath unfolding into breath
    Is the lotus
    Outstretched
      Radiance
      Unfurled
      10-fingered
        Gem:
    A jeweled
        Transect
    Of heart
      To beated pulse
    Of tender
      Tendrils
    Collapsed and breathing
      Rebirth from the decay
      Of seeded discarded
        Fruits
Strewn like constellations
    From the eye
      To find home
        Again
        As if it was always there.

1640

What is untold Truth
   Held
   As a potential
Of thunder
   To void,
Electric
   Lightning into
The behind, always
   Lagging,
Absorbed into
   Nothingness
Not as
   An Absolute
But as
An archaic stereotype
    Of the abyss
    Of emptiness
    That holds
    Your potential
    And Truth
    Hostage
      Always?

1641

So, what was awakened
   In the touch, tenderness
From you
   Before the roar?

The lion snarled,
   Teeth showing,
   Smiling back
To you
   Truth.

1642

Vague imprints
   Were left
 As once
    Glowing potential,
     Embers
    To be rekindled
   As one
   Galaxy
     Into the next,
    And I must
    Remember
    It is me
      Folding into me
      Again.

1643

In a dimensional
    Shift,
And the perspective
Is slanted
    Such that pen to paper
    Lacks the fundamental
Aspect,
    The grounding
    Is now rooted
    With head
    Back home
        In the stars.

1644

Rooted and below
   Is an echo
Of who I was,
      Untold to you
         Now,
But captive and crested
     In history's
Tomes,
    As reference
       Always
     To learn and teach.

1645

If it all began
  Before you blew
  An exhale,
Would it be true
  Or would it be
   Tethered,
    Tied and bolted
To the colors,
   Now unforeseen
   And untouched,
But known to me
  As life
    Itself,
     Nothing more,
     Nothing less,
    Always?

1646

The moonlit bliss
    Of the heart
Blinks, tears and closes
    Lid to exchange
Currency
    That truly
Lacks orbit, gravity
    And fullness of cycles—
Apparently eclipsing
    Every exhale
Such that inspiration
    Lacks
Depth, constellations
    And the vivid
    Dotted matrix
Of all that began
      Before the first exhale and after
Separation of ego
    Into duality
As the wholeness
    Feigned into
One stellar eclipse
     Of the crowning Truth.

1647

Variegated winds
   Of untruth
  Rooted and seeded
Into emboldened
    Colors, tones
     To distract
From tongue furled
    And curled,
     Rolled into tomorrow
As a tight-fisted hand
     Of untold stories
    Separated from others
    Far from dancing
    In the dark
  Under stars of a constellation
      Of constraint
    Such that
    You fold into
    It further
    As the ego
Strengthens its dance
  Like the archer
  In the sky
 Poised and ready
To grip
And almost molest
  Truly
   The Truth of the unmaskable
      Light.

1648

Parameters of day and night
   Are nothing more
  Nor less
    Than
The absolving of lightning
     Into ocean
  Waves too high
    To know
   Folding back into self
     Not as eye of the storm
   But as always
     Still
    In this blink
     And waking
       Glance
    From the constellation
       With hidden coded
      Hymns
        Singing
      In the blessed divine
       Lament
         Of awakened Truth.

1649

No longer
    The stellar elliptical
        Eclipse,
  Shadows
      Held long
      At noon
    Denotes not
        Archetypes
        Of light and dark
      But time
        Unfolding
        As a hidden
      Aspect
          Held in tow
            Too long.

1650

The expanse of golden
    Radiance,
Palm to palm,
  Brow to brow,
  And what is seen
    As a disrobement?
  And what is
    Touched
      As a cloak?

1651

The proper term for love
   Is neither word nor phrase,
  But potential, held and unfurled
     As sacred expanse of heart
       To heart
     And electric magnetic pulse
    Coming in
        As a wave of raw surrender
       Into ecstasy:
       Mysterious and known
      As my constellation
       Points
         To the pith of things.

Into the galaxy
   Before the folding
      Into the black hole—
          And, inverted out,
     Backwards breech birth
      And stillborn no longer
        Nor held as a potent miscarriage
        In the second trimester—
       God forbid, the last,
      But received as life breathing
        Sweetness of the known,
         Of what is always recognized,
      And held too close to
     Be expressed and trusted.

What is obvious and evident
       Is swatted from the eye's span
         Or arced midnight sky
        As asteroids, meteorites or seeming UFOs swarming
         Into the decay
       To know

This satellite in trajectory to implode
   Is neither in despair
   Nor stamped
     With man-made destruction:
    Inane radio signals of antiquated TV shows, outdated
    Perspective like atom bombs
     20 years ago sent off to explode
      In this space,
      So, one may decree it was never there,
       As after the detonation,
     Nothing is evident.

Apparently
   The purpose brings it closer to you
 So, all will be told,
     Not as an astronaut
       Coming back
        From the vortex,
      But as Truth,
      Evident and abundant
        In its simple elegance.

1652

In a random moment
　As if
　A random note
　　Seemingly
　From Miles' trumpet
　　Only because
　The sense and order
　　Is known
　　As a current
　　　Of raw, turbulent
　　　　Raging below
　　　A seemingly calm
　　　　Reflected moon,
　　　Yet no sense
　　　　Of how or why
　　　　　Gravity's pull
　　　　Opens
　　　　　And closes
　　　　　It all.

1653

Germination
  Postponed
    Is not forfeiture,
    Rather the breathing
      In and out,
        The exhale
      Of moist, unfurled
        Fertility
      Of sacredness of space
        Held close to the heart
        In the widest
        Of open expanse
      Like radiance
        In the touch,
          The awakening
          Of seeing, knowing
            And decoding
          Before the inhalation
          Of it all.

1654

Tendrils
  Have not only grown
  From seeds
    Planted,
   Haphazardly blown
    By the wind
    Into less than optimal
     Seasons
      And soil,
     Arid ecstasy,
      Searing heat
       For northern
      Conifers
       Renders
      A contradiction
        Of sorts,
       Actually death postponed
        Into a dormant
       Sealed freight
        Of desiccated potential
       Only until
      Plowed under
   It rose
  Into your heart
     For me to see
    All over
     Again.

1655

When perspective is peeled
    From abundance,
Reaped and touched
From nothing
    More than Truth,
Wisdom reveals its own
    Pithy sweet taste
      Of Oneness:
Ripe bounty of harvest
    In droughts of despair
      From all
The healing,
    And now
The contemplation,
    The plan in the grid work.

    The course will
      Steer all
    With plentitude
      In the seasons,
Dowsing the hate, venom,
    And greed,
And now knowing the clouds
    Obscured
      The radiance
Of fertility
    Not as a passing in the wind
    But like the darkest boldest
      Moment,
      Before the miscarriage
        Of justice is rectified.

1656

Abundance
   Is neither bounty
  Hoarded
    Nor treasury notes
  Counterfeited.

In the absence of exploited glory's
   Reflection,
 Narcissistic dominance
 And greed, abundance
   Is the heart
   Having unfolded,
     Humming with all
     The true infinite possibilities
     Of tender loving touch
       Of the Divine
       Through wind, rustled leaves,
       Rain melting sweat on the skin,
         Topless and above
         The grace of God opens
         Sky to earth
          Such that the deep enigma,
             The deepest mystery of the true feminine
             Unfolding lacks the dishonesty
             Of false currents
             And distorted constellations projecting
             And dissecting, manipulating
               In the wonderment and awe.

It now stills, as always,
       Such that shimmers and vibrancy
          Finally locate you and know
            That you are my Southern Cross, my North Star
              That could not be
                If the shelter of my arms and heart
                  Could not arc a place

        For the tenderness of yourself
        To come home to me again,
        And to know my heart is safe and loved
            In the palm of your hand,
                Heart to heart,
            And no longer the gap
                Between bodies, mind, and the always
                    On a hill at sunset.

And so the Southern Cross
    Will always carry me home
        To our hearth,
            Always,
    And the deep riddle of Truth that I bear
        Will always steer back
    Into our grounded selves
        Such that neither
            Will ever be lost again.
            Never.

1657

Witnessing in peace
    The solitude
   Of other's interlaced
    And woven
  Into plaids lacking
     Sword of Truth
    Touched by
      Muted vibrancy
     That distorts
    The distance,
     The angle
       Into perspective.

And with deep gratitude

Other poetry titles by Wendy E. Slater:

Full Circle Undivided, *Poems-Volume 1*

Into the Hearth, *Poems-Volume 14*

Of the Flame, *Poems-Volume 15*

The Perspective of Constellation, *Poems-Volume 17*

Visit Wendy E. Slater's website
www.traduka.com

www.ingramcontent.com/pod-product-compliance
Lightning Source LLC
Chambersburg PA
CBHW051807100526
44592CB00016B/2600